Meet The Chef

IG. @OLIVIAHERTZOG

RAW FOOD IS A GREAT WAY TO GET THE MOST OUT OF YOUR FOOD AND TO ENSURE THAT YOU ARE GETTING THE MOST NUTRIENTS POSSIBLE. WITH THAT BEING SAID I DON'T THINK YOU HAVE TO EAT ONLY RAW VEGAN FOOD IN ORDER TO BENEFIT IMMENSELY FROM EATING SOME RAW FOOD MEALS!

MY DESIRE FOR YOU IS TO CHOOSE RAW FOODS FOR THE LOVE OF THEM AND FOR THE LOVE OF YOU. YOU DESERVE THE ABSOLUTE BEST FOOD YOU CAN PREPARE. I HOPE THIS BOOK WILL HELP YOU FALL EVER MORE DEEPLY IN LOVE WITH LIVING, PLANT BASED FOODS!

~ Olivia Hertzog

Kitchen Equipment

HERE'S MY LIST OF RECOMMEND PRODUCTS TO MAKE YOUR
RAW VEGAN FOOD PREPPING THAT MUCH MORE FUN (TRULY,
THE PROPER TOOLS MAKE THE JOURNEY SO MUCH EASIER!)

JUICER: MY JUICER IS A <u>NAMA J2 JUICER</u>. I HAVE TESTED MANY JUICERS OUT OVER
THE YEARS AND THIS JUICER IS BY FAR MY FAVORITE! YOU CAN ORDER YOUR OWN HERE
AND FEEL FREE TO USE MY COUPON CODE TO SAVE $50+

COUPON CODE: OH10

BLENDER: I USE A <u>VITAMIX E310 EXPLORIAN BLENDER</u>. I LOVE VITAMIX AS A BRAND!
BEST BLENDER AND TRULY WORTH THE INVESTMENT—I KNOW VITAMIX'S TO HAVE
LASTED WELL OVER A DECADE WITH CONSISTENT USE.

DEHYDRATOR: I USE AN <u>EXCALIBUR 9 TRAY DEHYDRATOR</u>. AGAIN, I BELIEVE
EXCALIBUR IS THE BEST ON THE MARKET. I HAVE TWO OF THEIR DEHYDRATORS—THE
FIRST OF WHICH IS STILL GOING ALMOST 9 YEARS STRONG!

SPIRALIZER: AND A TOOL I PERSONALLY CAN'T LIVE WITHOUT (I USE IT
LITERALLY EVERY DAY): <u>MY HANDHELD SPIRALIZER</u>. THERE ARE LOTS OF THESE
AVAILABLE BUT THIS SMALL, HANDHELD SPIRALIZER HAS BEEN MY CONSTANT
COMPANION FOR A LONG TIME!

Contents

Contents

Contents

Contents

JUICES
& Smoothies

Apple Pear Juice

+ PREP TIME
10 MINUTES

INGREDIENTS

3 PEARS
3 APPLES
OPTIONAL ADD ONS: LEMON, LIME, GINGER

ABC Juice

+ PREP TIME
10 MINUTES

INGREDIENTS

5 APPLES
2 SMALL BEETS
3 CARROTS

Apple Carrot Ginger

+ PREP TIME
10 MINUTES

INGREDIENTS

6 APPLES
3 CARROTS
1 INCH OF FRESH GINGER

Green Juice

+ PREP TIME
10 MINUTES

INGREDIENTS

7 GREEN APPLES
2 STALKS OF CELERY
3 CUPS SPINACH
1 LEMON
ADD ONS OR INGREDIENT REPLACEMENTS:
GINGER, PARSLEY, SWISS CHARD, KALE, LIME

Strawberry Lemonade

+ PREP TIME
5 MINUTES

INGREDIENTS

8OZ WATER
6 DEGLET DATES
JUICE OF 1 LEMON
1 WHOLE CONTAINER OF STRAWBERRIES
(ABOUT 2 1/2 CUPS)

PROCESS

BLEND AND ENJOY!
*OPTION TO ADD A BANANA OR TWO FOR
MORE OF A CREAMY SMOOTHIE CONSISTENCY.

Berry Smoothie

+ PREP TIME
5 MINUTES

INGREDIENTS

12 OZ. WATER
10 DEGLET DATES (OR 5 MEDJOOL DATES,
OR 3 TBSP DATE PASTE)
1 CUP BLACKBERRIES
2 CUPS STRAWBERRIES
5 FROZEN BANANAS

PROCESS

BLEND AND ENJOY!

Chocolate Peanut Butter Banana Smoothie

+ PREP TIME
5 MINUTES

INGREDIENTS

8 OZ WATER
8 DEGLET DATES
5 BANANAS
2 TBSP PEANUT BUTTER
2 TBSP CACAO POWDER

PROCESS

BLEND AND ENJOY!

Watermelon Lemonade Smoothie

+ PREP TIME   + SERVINGS
10 MINUTES   1-2 PEOPLE

INGREDIENTS

ONE FULL PITCHER OF WATERMELON (64OZ PITCHER)
1/4 CUP FRESH MINT
JUICE OF 1/2 A LEMON

PROCESS

BLEND AND ENJOY!

Sunshine Smoothie

+ PREP TIME
5 MINUTES

INGREDIENTS

JUICE OF 3 NAVEL ORANGES
1 CUP FROZEN MANGOS
1 1/2 CUPS FRESH STRAWBERRIES

PROCESS

BLEND AND ENJOY!

Chocolate Protein Powder

+ PREP TIME
5 MINUTES

+ SERVINGS
10 SCOOPS

INGREDIENTS

2 TBSP RAW PUMPKIN SEEDS
2 TBSP HEMP SEEDS
2 TBSP FLAX SEEDS
2 TSP CHIA SEEDS
2 TBSP RAW CAROB (OR CACAO!) POWDER

PROCESS

BLEND ALL TOGETHER UNTIL IT FORMS A POWDER. PUT IT IN A JAR OR CONTAINER AND ADD A TEASPOON OR TABLESPOON TO YOUR NEXT SMOOTHIE.

Snickerdoodle Smoothie

+ PREP TIME
5 MINUTES

INGREDIENTS

8OZ WATER
8 DEGLET DATES
1 TSP CINNAMON
PINCH OF VANILLA BEAN
1 TBSP ALMOND BUTTER
2 FRESH BANANAS
3 FROZEN BANANAS

PROCESS

BLEND AND ENJOY!

Chocolate Strawberry Peanut Butter Smoothie

+ PREP TIME
5 MINUTES

INGREDIENTS

8OZ WATER
8 DEGLET DATES
1 TBSP PEANUT BUTTER
1 TBSP CACAO POWDER
3 BANANAS
1 CUP FROZEN STRAWBERRIES

PROCESS

BLEND AND ENJOY!

Banana Maca Smoothie

+ PREP TIME
5 MINUTES

INGREDIENTS

8OZ WATER
8 DEGLET DATES
2 TSP MACA POWDER
1 TBSP GROUND FLAX
2 FRESH BANANAS
3 FROZEN BANANAS

PROCESS

BLEND AND ENJOY!

Orange Creamsicle Smoothie

+ PREP TIME
5 MINUTES

INGREDIENTS

3 NAVEL ORANGES (MAKE SURE TO PICK OUT
THE SEEDS IF THERE ARE ANY)
4 BANANAS
1 TBSP MAPLE SYRUP
1 TBSP UNSWEETENED COCONUT
1 CUP WATER

PROCESS

BLEND AND ENJOY!

Green Tea Matcha Smoothie Bowl

+ PREP TIME
10 MINUTES

INGREDIENTS

4 FROZEN BANANAS
5 DEGLET DATES
2 TSP MATCHA POWDER
TINY BIT OF WATER

PROCESS

1. BLEND

2. TOP WITH WHATEVER YOU LOVE! I LOVE MY RAW GRANOLA, CACAO NIBS, FRESH BLUEBERRIES, DRIZZLE OF MACADAMIA NUT BUTTER, AND A DRIZZLE OF MAPLE SYRUP.

Lemon Creme Pie Smoothie Bowl

+ PREP TIME
10 MINUTES

INGREDIENTS

8 DEGLET DATES
4 FROZEN BANANAS
2 TBSP COCONUT CREAM
LEMON ZEST FROM ABOUT 1/4 OF A LEMON
TINY BIT OF WATER

PROCESS

1. BLEND

2. TOP WITH (AS ALWAYS) WHATEVER YOU LOVE! I ALMOST ALWAYS LOVE TO ADD MY RAW GRANOLA. I ALSO LOVE ADDING SHREDDED COCONUT, BLUEBERRIES, LEMON ZEST AND A DRIZZLE OF MAPLE SYRUP TO THIS BOWL!

Lemon Blueberry Smoothie

+ PREP TIME
5 MINUTES

INGREDIENTS

3 BANANAS
8 DEGLET DATES
3/4 CUP BLUEBERRIES
JUICE AND ZEST OF 1/2 A LEMON
1 CUP WATER

PROCESS

BLEND AND ENJOY!

My Favorite Green Smoothie

+ PREP TIME
5 MINUTES

INGREDIENTS

8 OZ WATER
8 DEGLET DATES
1/2 INCH CHUNK OF FRESH GINGER
1 TBSP DAILY GREEN BOOST
2 FRESH BANANAS
3 FROZEN BANANAS

PROCESS

BLEND AND ENJOY!

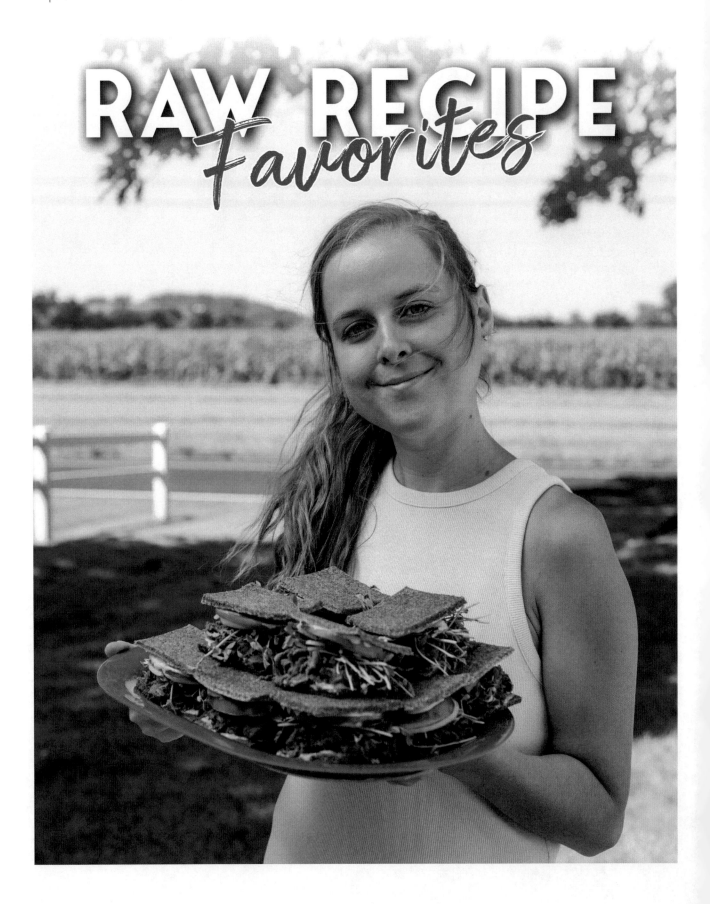

RAW RECIPE
Favorites

Raw Wraps

+ SERVINGS	+ PREP TIME	+ DEHYDRATE
2 PEOPLE	25 MINUTES	6-8 HOURS

INGREDIENTS

3 LARGE BELL PEPPERS

2 ROMA TOMATOES

2 TBSP WATER

1 TBSP SMOKED PAPRIKA

DASH OF SALT

2 TBSP PSYLLIUM HUSK

PROCESS

1. IN A HIGH SPEED BLENDER TOSS ALL THE INGREDIENTS EXCEPT THE PSYLLIUM HUSK. BLEND THOROUGHLY.

2. THEN TOSS IN THE PSYLLIUM AND BLEND AGAIN ON HIGH SPEED FOR ANOTHER 10 SECONDS. DIVIDE IN HALF AND SPREAD EVENLY AND THINLY ON TWO NONSTICK BAKING SHEETS. DEHYDRATE AT 115F FOR 6-8 HOURS UNTIL DRY BUT STILL PLIABLE.

3. (EXACT DEHYDRATING TIME WILL VARY DEPENDING ON HOW EFFICIENT YOUR DEHYDRATOR IS, HOW THICK/THIN YOU SPREAD THE WRAPS, ETC SO KEEP AN EYE ON THEM UNTIL YOU GET A FEEL FOR HOW ITS DONE!)

Sour Cream

+ SERVINGS
4-5 PEOPLE

+ PREP TIME
30 MINUTES

INGREDIENTS

1 CUP SOAKED AND PEELED ALMONDS
1 CUP WATER
3 CLOVES OF GARLIC
1 WHOLE LEMON
3 TBSP APPLE CIDER VINEGAR
1/2 TSP SALT

PROCESS

1. SOAK ALMONDS OVERNIGHT. AFTER SOAKING, PEEL THE SKINS OFF THE ALMONDS. THE SKIN WILL COME OFF PRETTY EASILY AFTER A NIGHT OF SOAKING

2. SLICE THE SKIN OFF OF YOUR LEMON AND CUT IN HALF TO REMOVE SEEDS

3. BLEND UNTIL NICE AND SMOOTH. IF YOU WANT THE SOUR CREAM A BIT THINNER AND RUNNIER, YOU CAN ADD A BIT MORE WATER. THEN ADD SOUR CREAM TO A SQUEEZE BOTTLE AND YOU'RE READY FOR TACO NIGHT!

Taco "Meat"

+ SERVINGS
2 PEOPLE

+ PREP TIME
15 MINUTES

+ DEHYDRATE
3-4 HOURS

INGREDIENTS

2 LARGE CARROTS
1 ROMA TOMATO
2 TSP GARLIC POWDER
1/2 CUP RAW SUNFLOWER SEEDS
1 TBSP LEMON JUICE
2 TSP CHILI POWDER
2 TSP CUMIN
1 TSP SWEET PAPRIKA
1/2 TSP SALT (OPTIONAL)

PROCESS

1. SOAK SUNFLOWER SEEDS FOR AT LEAST 4 HOURS

2. TOSS EVERYTHING IN A FOOD PROCESSOR. ONCE IT'S ALL WELL COMBINED TRANSFER TO A NONSTICK BAKING SHEET.

3. POP IN THE DEHYDRATOR FOR 3 HOURS OR SO AT 115F. (THIS ISN'T ABSOLUTELY NECESSARY OF COURSE BUT IT DOES ALLOW SOME OF THE MOISTURE TO BE RELEASED--AND IT GETS JUST EVER SO SLIGHTLY CRUNCHY)

Alfredo

+ SERVINGS
2 PEOPLE

+ PREP TIME
15 MINUTES

INGREDIENTS

2 12OZ PACKAGES OF KELP NOODLES
1 CUP SOAKED RAW MACADAMIA NUTS
1 CUP OF WATER
4 TBSP NUTRITIONAL YEAST
JUICE OF 1 LEMON
1 MEDJOOL DATE
2 TSP GARLIC POWDER
1 TSP ONION POWDER
DASH OF SALT (OPTIONAL)
DASH OF BLACK PEPPER

PROCESS

1. FOR THE KELP NOODLES EMPTY THE PACKAGES INTO A BIG BOWL. SOME PEOPLE LIKE TO PREPARE THEM BY SOAKING THEM IN HOT WATER. I PREFER THE FASTER METHOD OF SPRINKLING SOME BAKING POWDER ALL OVER THE NOODLES AND THEN DUMPING VINEGAR OVER THE TOP. IT CREATES A FIZZY REACTION THAT'S JUST FUN (LOL) AND SOFTENS THEM UP IN JUST A MINUTE! IF THEY'RE NOT TOTALLY SOFT DO A SECOND ROUND OF BAKING SODA/VINEGAR. THEN TAKE TO THE SINK AND RINSE THE NOODLES OFF.

2. TOSS ALL THE REST OF THE INGREDIENTS IN A BLENDER AND BLEND UNTIL SUPER SMOOTH AND CREAMY. THEN POUR OVER THE KELP NOODLES. TOP WITH A BIT MORE FRESH CRACKED BLACK PEPPER, A SPRINKLE OF FRESH OR DEHYDRATED PARSLEY AND ENJOY!

Pad Thai

+ SERVINGS
2 PEOPLE

+ PREP TIME
15 MINUTES

INGREDIENTS

1 12OZ PACKAGE OF KELP NOODLES
1 LARGE NOODLED ZUCCHINI
1 RED BELL PEPPER
2 CUPS OF BROCCOLI
2 TBSP COCONUT AMINOS
JUICE OF 2 LIMES
2 TBSP MAPLE SYRUP
2 TSP GARLIC POWDER
1 TSP ONION POWDER
2 TBSP PEANUT BUTTER

PROCESS

1. FOR THE KELP NOODLES EMPTY THE PACKAGE INTO A BIG BOWL. SOME PEOPLE LIKE TO PREPARE THEM BY SOAKING THEM IN HOT WATER. I PREFER THE FASTER METHOD OF SPRINKLING SOME BAKING POWDER ALL OVER THE NOODLES AND THEN DUMPING VINEGAR OVER THE TOP. IT CREATES A FIZZY REACTION THAT'S JUST FUN AND SOFTENS THEM UP IN JUST A MINUTE! IF THEY'RE NOT TOTALLY SOFT DO A SECOND ROUND OF BAKING SODA/VINEGAR. THEN TAKE TO THE SINK AND RINSE THE NOODLES OFF.

2. THEN SPIRALIZE THE ZUCCHINI AND TOSS THAT IN WITH THE KELP NOODLES. CHOP UP YOUR PEPPER AND BROCCOLI AND TOSS IN WITH THE NOODLES.

3. COMBINE THE REST OF THE INGREDIENTS FOR THE SAUCE. YOU CAN BLEND IT IN A BLENDER, OR JUST WHISK IT TOGETHER. POUR OVER THE VEGGIES AND NOODLES AND ALLOW TO SIT AND MARINATE FOR AT LEAST 2-3 HOURS. SOMETIMES I LIKE TO TRANSFER IT ALL TO A DEHYDRATOR SHEET TO WARM IT UP FOR A BIT. SOMETIMES I JUST SKIP THAT AND EAT IT AT ROOM TEMPERATURE.

4. ENJOY!

Rawtee'd Veggies

+ PREP TIME	+ SERVINGS	+ DEHYDRATE TIME
10 MINUTES	1-2 DISHES	4 HOURS

INGREDIENTS

IN A BOWL THINLY CHOP:
1 SMALL SWEET ONION
2 RED BELL PEPPERS (OR WHATEVER COLOR BELL PEPPERS YOU HAVE/LOVE)
1 LARGE TOMATO

MARINATE WITH:
1/4 CUP COCONUT AMINOS
1 TBSP FRESH GINGER
FRESH CRACKED BLACK PEPPER

PROCESS

1. ALLOW TO MARINATE FOR 10 MINUTES OR SO THEN TRANSFER TO A NONSTICK SHEET FOR YOUR DEHYDRATOR AND DEHYDRATE AT 115F FOR 4 HOURS.

2. YOU CAN USE THESE VEGGIES FOR TACOS, A PIZZA, TO STUFF IN A WRAP, TOSS ON A VEGGIE BURGER OR TO TOP A SALAD!

Raw Vegan Chex Mix

+ PREP TIME	+ SERVINGS	+ DEHYDRATE TIME
10 MINUTES	6-8 PEOPLE	8 HOURS

INGREDIENTS

1 CUP MACADAMIA NUTS (ALMONDS OR CASHEWS WOULD BE GREAT AS WELL!)
1 1/2 CUPS PUMPKIN SEEDS
1 1/2 CUPS SUNFLOWER SEEDS
4 TBSP COCONUT AMINOS
1/2 CUP CHOPPED SUNDRIED TOMATOES
2 TSP GARLIC POWDER
2 TSP ONION POWDER
1 TSP CHILI POWDER
2 TBSP WATER

PROCESS

1. DUMP THAT ALTOGETHER IN A BIG BOWL AND MIX IT TOGETHER.

2. ONCE EVERYTHING IS THOROUGHLY COATED AND WELL COMBINED SPREAD ON A DEHYDRATOR SHEET AND DEHYDRATE FOR 8 HOURS AT 115F AND THEN ENJOY!

Everything Bagel Crackers

+ PREP TIME
15 MINUTES

+ SERVINGS
3 PEOPLE

+ DEHYDRATE TIME
10 HOURS

INGREDIENTS

1/2 CUP GROUND FLAX
3/4 CUP WHITE SESAME SEEDS
1/2 CUP BLACK SESAME SEEDS
2 TBSP POPPY SEEDS
1 TBSP ONION FLAKES
1 TSP GARLIC POWDER
1 TSP ONION POWDER
1/2 TSP SALT
1/2 TSP BLACK PEPPER
1 1/2 TBSP MAPLE SYRUP
1 CUP WATER

PROCESS

1. MIX EVERYTHING THOROUGHLY AND ALLOW TO SIT AND "GEL" TOGETHER FOR 10 MINUTES.

2. ONCE GELLED SPREAD THE MIXTURE EVENLY ON A NONSTICK SHEET AND DEHYDRATE FOR 5 HOURS AT 115F.

3. THEN FLIP OVER THE NONSTICK SHEET. SCORE CRACKERS TO PREFERRED SIZE. AND DEHYDRATE THE OTHER SIDE FOR ANOTHER 5-7 HOURS UNTIL CRISPY.

Cheezy Kale Chips

+ PREP TIME
15 MINUTES

+ SERVINGS
2 PEOPLE

+ DEHYDRATE TIME
3 1/2 HOURS

INGREDIENTS

1LB KALE
3 CLOVES OF GARLIC
1/3 CUP OF NUTRITIONAL YEAST
1 1/2 TSP BLACK PEPPER
2 TSP PAPRIKA
1/4 CUP HEMP SEEDS
2 TBSP COCONUT AMINOS

PROCESS

1. DE-STEM KALE AND ROUGHLY CHOP IT BUT DON'T CHOP TOO SMALL OR YOU'LL HAVE KALE CRUMBLES INSTEAD OF CHIPS.

2. BLEND UP THE REMAINING INGREDIENTS IN A BLENDER, THEN MASSAGE OVER THE KALE. REALLY WORK IT INTO THE KALE WITH YOUR HANDS.

3. THEN PLACE DIRECTLY ON A DEHYDRATOR SHEET (OR TWO) AND DEHYDRATE AT 115F FOR ABOUT 3 1/2 HOURS. MAKE SURE TO SPREAD THINLY AND NOT LAYERED SO THEY CAN DEHYDRATE EVENLY AND CRISP UP.

4. DEHYDRATE TIME WILL VARY DEPENDING ON THE TEMPERATURE AND HUMIDITY LEVEL IN YOUR HOME. YOU MAY NEED TO DEHYDRATE LONGER.

Cool Ranch Kale Chips

+ PREP TIME
20 MINUTES

+ SERVINGS
2 PEOPLE

+ DEHYDRATE TIME
3 1/2 HOURS

INGREDIENTS

1LB KALE

FOR THE RANCH DRESSING:
1/2 CUP HEMP SEEDS
1 CUP CHOPPED AND PEELED ZUCCHINI
2 MEDJOOL DATES
1 TBSP LEMON JUICE
2 TSP APPLE CIDER VINEGAR
2 TSP GARLIC POWDER
1 TSP ONION POWDER
DASH OF SALT
1/2 CUP WATER

THEN STIR IN:
1 TBSP ONION FLAKES
1 TBSP FRESHLY CHOPPED PARSLEY
1 TBSP FRESHLY CHOPPED DILL
SOME FRESH CRACKED BLACK PEPPER
DASH OF CAYENNE

PROCESS

1. DE-STEM KALE AND ROUGHLY CHOP IT BUT DON'T CHOP TOO SMALL OR YOU'LL HAVE KALE CRUMBLES INSTEAD OF CHIPS.

2. BLEND RANCH DRESSING INGREDIENTS ALL TOGETHER IN A HIGH SPEED BLENDER.

3. LATHER THE SAUCE ON TOP, MASSAGING IT WITH YOUR HANDS, SPREAD EVENLY ON TWO DEHYDRATOR TRAYS.

4. POP IN THE DEHYDRATOR AT 115F FOR 3 HOURS OR SO (DEPENDING ON HOW THINLY YOU SPREAD THEM ON THE DEHYDRATOR SHEET) AND YOU HAVE A SALTY, CRUNCHY TREAT!

Egg Salad

+ PREP TIME
20 MINUTES

+ SERVINGS
2 PEOPLE

+ SET TIME
20 MINUTES

INGREDIENTS

1 CUP MACADAMIA NUTS
1/4 CUP WATER
1 TBSP LEMON JUICE
1 TSP TURMERIC POWDER
3/4 TSP BLACK SALT (THIS IS AN ESSENTIAL
INGREDIENT FOR THAT "EGGY" FLAVOR)
1 CLOVE OF GARLIC
1 STALK CELERY
FRESH GROUND BLACK PEPPER

PROCESS

1. START BY SOAKING THE MACADAMIA
   NUTS OVER NIGHT (OR AT THE VERY
   LEAST FOR 3 HOURS).

2. THEN TOSS ALL THE INGREDIENTS
   EXCEPT FOR THE CELERY IN A BLENDER.
   BLEND IT ALL UP BUT ALLOW FOR SOME
   TEXTURE: SMALL CHUNKS OF NUTS.
   IT'S BETTER THAT IT'S NOT ENTIRELY
   PULVERIZED.

3. CHOP UP THE STALK OF CELERY AND
   PUT IT ALL IN A BOWL TO MARINATE
   TOGETHER IN THE FRIDGE FOR A FEW
   HOURS.

Raw Mozzarella

+ PREP TIME	+ SERVINGS	+ SET TIME
15 MINUTES	4 PEOPLE	2 HOURS

INGREDIENTS

1 CUP MACADAMIA NUTS (OR CASHEWS IF YOU PREFER)
2 CLOVES OF GARLIC
1 WHOLE LEMON (PEELED AND SEEDS REMOVED)
2 TBSP APPLE CIDER VINEGAR
1/2 TSP SALT
1/2 TSP WHITE PEPPER
1 CUP OF WATER

2 TBSP OF A LIGHT PSYLLIUM HUSK (I LIKE THE BRAND HEALTHWORKS. YOU WANT A LIGHT PSYLLIUM BECAUSE SOME OF THEM ARE DARKER AND YOU DON'T REALLY WANT YOUR MOZZARELLA TO COME OUT A BROWNISH COLOR—WILL TASTE FINE, JUST WON'T LOOK AS NICE.)

PROCESS

1. BEGIN BY SOAKING 1 CUP OF MACADAMIA NUTS OVERNIGHT THE NEXT DAY DRAIN OFF THE WATER FROM THE MACADAMIA NUTS AND TOSS THE NUTS IN YOUR BLENDER WITH ALL THE IN GREDIENTS EXCEPT THE PSYLLIUM HUSK.

2. THEN ADD IN 2 TBSP OF A LIGHT PSYLLIUM HUSK. BLEND UP THE PSYLLIUM HUSK WITH THE REST OF THE MOZZARELLA INGREDIENTS. IT SHOULD BE PRETTY THICK.

3. TRANSFER TO A BOWL OR A GLASS OR (IF YOU HAVE IT!) SOME SORT OF CHEESE MOLD. I JUST USE A NICE ROUNDED BOWL. FLATTEN AND SMOOTH IT OUT NICELY IN WHATEVER YOU'RE USING. THE CHEESE WILL TAKE ON THE FORM OF WHATEVER CONTAINER YOU USE.

4. ALLOW TO SIT IN THE FRIDGE TO SET UP FOR SEVERAL HOURS. AND THEN IT'S GOOD TO SLICE AND EAT!

Raw-Men

+ SERVINGS	+ PREP TIME	+ DEHYDRATE
2 PEOPLE	30 MINUTES	2 HOURS

INGREDIENTS

FOR THE "BROTH"/MARINADE:
JUICE OF 2 LIMES
1 TBSP TAHINI
2 TBSP COCONUT AMINOS
1/4 CUP FRESH OJ
1 TBSP MAPLE SYRUP

THEN CHOP TO YOUR DESIRED SIZE:
2 RED BELL PEPPER
1 SMALL SWEET ONION
1 DOZEN STALKS OF ASPARAGUS (YOU
COULD USE BROCCOLI INSTEAD IF YOU
PREFER!)

2 LARGE ZUCCHINIS (OR 3 ENGLISH
CUCUMBERS)

PROCESS

1. START BY COMBINING THE MARINADE INGREDIENTS IN A BIG BOWL AND WHISK THEM ALL TOGETHER

2. ONCE OTHER INGREDIENTS ARE CHOPPED, TOSS ALL THOSE THINGS IN THE BOWL WITH THE MAR-
    INADE. MIX IT TOGETHER REALLY WELL AND THEN PUT ON A NONSTICK SHEET IN THE DEHYDRATOR
    FOR 2 HOURS.

3. ONCE THAT'S DONE SPIRALIZE 2 LARGE ZUCCHINI'S OR 3 ENGLISH CUCUMBERS. MIX IN THE DEHY-
    DRATED VEGGIES. POUR THE REMAINING "BROTH"/MARINADE OVER TOP AND DONE!

Mushroom Stroganoff

+ SERVINGS
2 PEOPLE

+ PREP TIME
20 MINUTES

INGREDIENTS

FOR THE MARINADE:
8OZ MUSHROOMS
1/4 CUP CHOPPED SWEET ONION
6 SPRIGS OF FRESH THYME
2 TBSP COCONUT AMINOS

FOR THE SAUCE:
1/4 CUP SPROUTED SUNFLOWER SEEDS
2 CLOVES OF GARLIC
1/4 TSP GROUND MUSTARD
1/2 TSP PAPRIKA
1 LEMON (PEELED)
1 TBSP APPLE CIDER VINEGAR
1/3 CUP WATER

1 MEDIUM/LARGE ZUCCHINI

PROCESS

1. ADD ALL MARINADE INGREDIENTS INTO A BOWL, MIX THEM UP AND LET THEM SIT.

2. BLEND ALL THE SAUCE INGREDIENTS

3. THEN PEEL AND NOODLE UP A MEDIUM/LARGE ZUCCHINI. TOSS THEM WITH THE SAUCE, TOP WITH THE MUSHROOM MIXTURE.

4. ADD A SPRINKLE OF FRESH PARSLEY, SOME MORE FRESH THYME AND SOME RED OR BLACK PEPPER AND DONE!

Raw Crackers

+ SERVINGS
2 PEOPLE

+ PREP TIME
20 MINUTES

+ DEHYDRATE
10 HOURS

INGREDIENTS

3 LARGE CARROTS
1 RED BELL PEPPER
1 STALK OF CELERY
2 TSP ONION POWDER
2 TSP GARLIC POWDER
2 TSP SMOKED PAPRIKA
2 TBSP ITALIAN SEASONING
2 TBSP FLAX SEEDS
1 TSP SALT (OPTIONAL)
1 TBSP SUNFLOWER SEEDS
1 TBSP PUMPKIN SEEDS

PROCESS

1. ROUGHLY CHOP THE VEGETABLES AND
   TOSS THEM IN A FOOD PROCESSOR.
   ADD ALL THE INGREDIENTS EXCEPT FOR
   THE SUNFLOWER AND PUMPKIN SEEDS.
   PROCESS UNTIL WELL COMBINED AND
   RELATIVELY SMOOTH. YOU WANT IT TO
   BE PRETTY WELL PROCESSED SO IT
   THICKENS AND GELS TOGETHER.

2. THEN ADD THE SUNFLOWER AND PUMP-
   KIN SEEDS AND PROCESS UNTIL THOSE
   ARE PRETTY WELL CHOPPED UP.

3. TRANSFER TO A NONSTICK BAKING
   SHEET OR A PIECE OF WAX PAPER AND
   PRESS IT INTO A SQUARE/RECTANGLE
   ABOUT 1/2 AN INCH THICK. DEHYDRATE
   AT 115F FOR ABOUT 4 HOURS.

4. THEN FLIP OFF THE NONSTICK SHEET
   AND SCORE THE CRACKERS INTO THE
   SIZE AND SHAPE YOU WANT THEM TO
   BE. DEHYDRATE AGAIN FOR ANOTHER 6
   HOURS OR SO UNTIL THEY'RE DRY LIKE
   CRACKERS!

Feta

+ SERVINGS
4 PERSON

+ PREP TIME
15 MINUTES

INGREDIENTS

1 CUP SOAKED AND PEELED ALMONDS
2 1/2 TBSP LEMON JUICE
1/4 TSP SALT

PROCESS

1. TOSS EVERYTHING IN THE FOOD PROCESSOR AND PULSE UNTIL IT LOOKS LIKE FETA!

2. THE MORE YOU PROCESS THE MORE IT WILL STICK TOGETHER LIKE A TRADITIONAL CLUMP OF FETA. BUT DON'T OVER PROCESS OR YOU'LL HAVE A SOUR ALMOND BUTTER.

SALADS
& Dressings

Sprout & Microgreen Salad

+ SERVINGS
2 PEOPLE

+ PREP TIME
15 MINUTES

INGREDIENTS

2 HEADS OF CHOPPED ROMAINE
1 BUNDLE OF CILANTRO
1 CUP SUNFLOWER MICROGREENS
1 CUP PEA SHOOTS
1 MEDIUM SIZED CUCUMBER
1 CUP OF MUSHROOMS
1/4 CUP ONION
1 CUP BROCCOLI SPROUTS
2 TBSP LENTIL SPROUTS
1/2 CUP CHOPPED TOMATOES

PROCESS

1. CHOP IT ALL TO YOUR DESIRED SIZE.
    PLACE IN A BOWL AND ENJOY!

Mean Green Salad

+ SERVINGS
2 PEOPLE

+ PREP TIME
15 MINUTES

INGREDIENTS

1-2 HEADS OF ROMAINE
1 HEAD OF BUTTER LETTUCE
1 1/2 CUPS OF CUCUMBER
1 CUP SNAP PEAS
1 HANDFUL OF FRESH BASIL
1/4 CUP FRESH THYME
1 MEDIUM SPIRALIZED ZUCCHINI
1/4 CUP ONION
1/3 CUP LENTIL SPROUTS
1 HANDFUL ALFALFA SPROUTS

PROCESS

1. CHOP IT ALL TO YOUR DESIRED SIZE,
    PLACE IN A BOWL AND ENJOY!

Raw Vegan Waldorf Salad

+ SERVINGS
2 PEOPLE

+ PREP TIME
20 MINUTES

INGREDIENTS

FOR THE SALAD:
4 CUPS OF ROMAINE
4 CUPS CHOPPED BROCCOLI
1/2 CUP RAISINS
3 STALKS OF CHOPPED CELERY
1/2 CUP CHOPPED WALNUTS
1 LARGE CHOPPED APPLE
1/2 A SMALL RED ONION SLICED UP

FOR THE "MAYO" DRESSING TOSS IN A BLENDER:
1/2 CUP SOAKED SUNFLOWER SEEDS
1/4 CUP CAULIFLOWER (OPTIONAL, REALLY)
1 CLOVE GARLIC
2 TBSP LEMON JUICE
1/2 TSP STONEGROUND MUSTARD
1 TBSP MAPLE SYRUP
1/4 CUP WATER
DASH OF SALT

PROCESS

1. CHOP UP ALL SALAD INGREDIENTS TO YOUR DESIRED SIZE. PLACE IN A BOWL

2. BLEND ALL DRESSING INGREDIENTS TO-GETHER UNTIL IT'S NICE AND SMOOTH THEN POUR OVER THE VEGGIE BOWL AND NICELY COAT EVERYTHING. SPREAD THAT MIXTURE OVER YOUR GREENS.

3. TOP WITH SOME SPROUTS, MICRO-GREENS, YOUR FAVORITE "TOPPINGS" AND DIG IN!

Raw Jackfruit Taco Meat

+ SERVINGS
2 PEOPLE

+ PREP TIME
15 MINUTES

+ SET TIME
2 HOURS

INGREDIENTS

1/2 LB OF JACKFRUIT
1/2 A PACKET OF ORGANIC TACO SEASONING BLEND
2 TBSP COCONUT AMINOS (OR LIME JUICE)

PROCESS

1. PUT THE JACKFRUIT IN A BOWL, TOSS THE COCONUT AMINOS IN THERE AND THE SEASONING AND MIX IT ALL UP!

2. I LIKE TO ALLOW THIS TO MARINATE FOR AT LEAST A COUPLE HOURS—THOUGH OVERNIGHT SEEMS EVEN BETTER.

Jackfruit Taco Salad

+ SERVINGS
2 PEOPLE

+ PREP TIME
20 MINUTES

INGREDIENTS

1 CUP CHOPPED SWISS CHARD
1/4 CUP CHOPPED CILANTRO
2 CUPS SPINACH
1/2 A CHOPPED CUCUMBER
1 MEDIUM SPIRALIZED ZUCCHINI
1/2 LB JACKFRUIT TACO "MEAT"
1/2 CUP CORN
1 MEDIUM TOMATO
2 TBSP RED ONION
DRIZZLE OF ALMOND SOUR CREAM

PROCESS

1. CHOP IT ALL TO YOUR DESIRED SIZE.
   PLACE IN A BOWL

2. TOP WITH ALMOND SOUR CREAM AND ENJOY

Seafood Salad

+ SERVINGS
2 PEOPLE

+ PREP TIME
20 MINUTES

TOP WITH:
1-2 NORI SHEETS
1/4 CUP DRIED WAKAME
1TSP SESAME SEEDS

INGREDIENTS

FOR THE SALAD:
4 CUPS ROMAINE
1 LARGE CUCUMBER
1-1 1/2 OUNCES OF REHYDRATED WAKAME
1/4 CUP CHOPPED DULSE
CHOP AND ADD ALL TO A BOWL.

FOR THE DRESSING:
2 TBSP TAHINI
PINCH OF FRESH GINGER
2 TSP MISO
1 TBSP APPLE CIDER VINEGAR
2 TSP AGAVE

PROCESS

1. SOAK WAKAME IN 2/3 CUPS OF WATER

2. CHOP ALL SALAD INGREDIENTS TO YOUR DESIRED SIZE, PLACE IN A BOWL

3. WHISK TOGETHER DRESSING INGREDIENTS AND TOP YOUR SALAD.

4. ADD 1-2 SHEETS OF CRUSHED NORI, AND MORE DRIED WAKAME FOR A LITTLE CRUNCH

5. AND A SPRINKLE OF SESAME SEEDS TO THE TOP AND ENJOY

Guacamole Salad

+ SERVINGS
2 PEOPLE

+ PREP TIME
15 MINUTES

INGREDIENTS

FOR THE SALAD:
4 CUPS CHOPPED ROMAINE
1/2 A SPIRALIZED ZUCCHINI
1/2 A CHOPPED CUCUMBER
2 TBSP CHOPPED ONION
1/2 CUP CHOPPED TOMATO

FOR THE GUACAMOLE:
1/2 CUP FINELY DICED TOMATO
2 TBSP FINELY CHOPPED ONION
JUICE OF 1 LEMON
2 LARGE AVOCADOS
1/4 CUP FINELY CHOPPED CILANTRO
PINCH OF SALT

PROCESS

1. CHOP UP ALL YOUR SALAD INGREDIENTS AND ADD THEM INTO A BOWL.

2. COMBINE YOUR GUACAMOLE INGREDIENTS AND PLACE ON TOP YOUR SALAD.

My Favorite Dressing

+ PREP TIME
5 MINUTES

+ SERVINGS
1 SALAD

INGREDIENTS

2 TBSP TAHINI
2 TBSP MAPLE SYRUP
2 TBSP LEMON JUICE (OR LIME JUICE OR APPLE CIDER VINEGAR)
2 TBSP COCONUT AMINOS

SHAKE OR WHISK IT UP AND SERVE!

Tahini Miso Dip

+ PREP TIME
5 MINUTES

+ SERVINGS
3 PEOPLE

INGREDIENTS

1/2 CUP TAHINI
1 1/2 TBSP MISO
2 TBSP APPLE CIDER VINEGAR
(OR LEMON JUICE)
2 TBSP MAPLE SYRUP
1/4 CUP WATER
1/2 A MEDIUM PEELED ZUCCHINI
(THIS IS TO BULK UP THE DIP. YOU CAN TOTALLY LEAVE IT OUT IF YOU WANT).

PLACE IT ALL IN A BLENDER AND BLEND UNTIL SMOOTH!

Raw Ketchup

+ PREP TIME
10 MINUTES

+ SERVINGS
3 PEOPLE

INGREDIENTS

IN A BLENDER TOSS:
1 CUP SUNDRIED TOMATOES
10 DEGLET DATES
2 CLOVES OF GARLIC
1/4 CUP APPLE CIDER VINEGAR
(OR LEMON JUICE)
1 TSP PAPRIKA
3/4 CUP CHOPPED TOMATOES

BLEND UNTIL NICE AND SMOOTH!

French Dressing

+ PREP TIME
10 MINUTES

+ SERVINGS
3 SALADS

INGREDIENTS

1 CUP TOMATOES
1 CUP PITTED DATES
1/3 CUP APPLE CIDER VINEGAR
(OR LEMON JUICE)
2 TSP PAPRIKA
2 TSP GARLIC POWDER
2 TSP ONION POWDER
WATER TO BLEND

BLEND AND ENJOY!

Guacamole

+ PREP TIME
5 MINUTES

+ SERVINGS
3 PEOPLE

INGREDIENTS

1/2 CUP FINELY DICED TOMATO
2 TBSP FINELY CHOPPED ONION
JUICE OF 1 LEMON
2 LARGE AVOCADOS
1/4 CUP FINELY CHOPPED CILANTRO
PINCH OF SALT

PROCESS

MIX THAT ALL TOGETHER AND DONE!
(YOUCOULD ALSO ALWAYS ADD FRESH OR POWDERED
GARLIC. LIME INSTEAD OF LEMON, BLACK PEPPER OR
RED PEPPER FLAKES--AS ALWAYS DO WHAT YOU LOVE
AND SOUNDS YUMMY!)

Honey Mustard Dressing

+ PREP TIME
10 MINUTES

+ SERVINGS
2 SALADS

INGREDIENTS

2 TBSP WHOLE GRAIN MUSTARD (I JUST BUY
AN ORGANIC BOTTLED MUSTARD USUALLY:
NOT TECHNICALLY RAW BUT EASIER THIS WAY)
4 TBSP TAHINI
6 MEDJOOL DATES
2 TBSP MAPLE SYRUP
2 CLOVES OF GARLIC
4 TBSP LEMON JUICE
1/2 TSP TURMERIC POWDER
1 CUP WATER
1/2 TSP SALT
DASH OF FRESH CRACKED BLACK PEPPER
BLEND IT ALL UP AND POUR OVER YOUR
FAVORITE SALAD OR USE AS A DIP FOR
WRAPS, ETC!

41

Raw Vegan Tzaziki Sauce

+ PREP TIME
10 MINUTES

+ SERVINGS
2 SALADS

INGREDIENTS

IN A BLENDER TOSS:
1/2 CUP SOAKED MACADAMIA NUTS (OR CASHEWS.
OR SUNFLOWER SEEDS—WHATEVER YOU PREFER)
2 CUPS PEELED CUCUMBER
JUICE OF 1 LEMON
2 CLOVES OF GARLIC
1/2 CUP CHOPPED SWEET ONION
1/3 CUP WATER TO BLEND (OR LESS OR MORE DE-
PENDING ON HOW THICK YOU WANT IT).
DASH OF SALT

BLEND THAT ALL UP THEN STIR IN:
1 TBSP DRIED DILL
1 TSP DRIED MINT
LOTS OF FRESH CRACKED BLACK PEPPER!

IT'S IDEAL IF YOU ALLOW IT TO SIT FOR
EVEN JUST A LITTLE WHILE SO THE FLAVORS
CAN MINGLE....
BUT IF YOU'RE TOO IMPATIENT, ENJOY!

Lovely Lime Dressing

+ PREP TIME
5 MINUTES

+ SERVINGS
1 SALAD

INGREDIENTS

JUICE OF 2 LIMES
2 TBSP TAHINI
5 MEDJOOL DATES
2 TSP APPLE CIDER VINEGAR
1 CLOVE OF GARLIC
1 TBSP COCONUT AMINOS
AND HALF A LARGE JALAPENO (IF YOU'RE INTO THE
HEAT. ;))

PROCESS

BLEND UNTIL WELL COMBINED! ENJOY ON
YOUR FAVORITE SALAD!

Creamy Buffalo Sauce

+ PREP TIME   + SERVINGS

5 MINUTES   2 SALADS

INGREDIENTS

1/2 CUP SOAKED CASHEWS
(OR MACADAMIA NUTS, OR HEMP SEEDS)
JUICE OF 1 LEMON
2 TBSP APPLE CIDER VINEGAR
2 CLOVES OF GARLIC
2 TBSP COCONUT AMINOS
7 DEGLET DATES
1 TSP SMOKED PAPRIKA
DASH OF CAYENNE
1/2 CUP WATER

PROCESS

BLEND IT ALL AND ENJOY!

Miso Ginger Dressing

+ PREP TIME   + SERVINGS

5 MINUTES   1 SALAD

INGREDIENTS

2 TBSP TAHINI
2 TBSP LIME JUICE
1 TBSP WHITE MISO PASTE
1 CLOVE OF GARLIC VERY FINELY CHOPPED
1 TINY CHUNK OF GINGER VERY FINELY CHOPPED
(ABOUT THE SIZE OF YOUR THUMBNAIL)
1 TBSP WATER (OR MORE IF YOU PREFER!)

PROCESS

WHISK THAT ALL TOGETHER AND POUR
OVER YOUR FAVORITE SALAD!

Orange Miso Dressing

+ PREP TIME   + SERVINGS

5 MINUTES   1 SALAD

INGREDIENTS

1 TBSP MISO
1/2 CUP ORANGE JUICE
2 TBSP TAHINI
2 CLOVES OF GARLIC
2 MEDJOOL DATES (OR 4 DEGLET DATES)

PROCESS

ADD IT ALL TO A BLENDER, BLEND AND ENJOY!

Teriyaki Sauce

+ PREP TIME   +SERVINGS

5 MINUTES   2 SALADS

INGREDIENTS

3 TBSP TAHINI
2 TBSP COCONUT AMINOS
2 CLOVES OF GARLIC
10 DEGLET DATES
1 TBSP MAPLE SYRUP
CHUNK OF GINGER THE SIZE OF YOUR
THUMBNAIL
1 TSP PAPRIKA

PROCESS

ADD AS LITTLE OR AS MUCH WATER AS YOU
WANT—DEPENDING ON HOW THICK YOU
WANT THE SAUCE. BLEND AND ENJOY!

DEHYDRATED
Gourmet

Raw Vegan Quiche

+ SERVINGS
4 PEOPLE

+ PREP TIME
30 MINUTES

+ DEHYDRATE
4 HOURS + 8 HOURS

INGREDIENTS

FOR THE CRUST:
1 CUP MACADAMIA NUTS SOAKED OVER-
NIGHT
3 TBSP FLAX MEAL
2 TSP NUTRITIONAL YEAST
1/4 TSP SALT
3 TBSP WATER
1 TBSP LEMON JUICE

FOR THE FILLING:
1 1/2 CUPS PEELED ZUCCHINI
1/4 CUP WATER
1 CUP MACADAMIA NUTS
2 TBSP WHITE MISO
2 TBSP LEMON JUICE
3 TBSP NUTRITIONAL YEAST
2 TSP PSYLLIUM HUSKS
1/2 TSP BLACK SALT (FOR THAT EGGY FLA-
VOR)
1/4 TSP TURMERIC POWDER TO GIVE IT THAT
YELLOW EGGY LOOK.

FOLD IN THESE INGREDIENTS:
2 CUPS CHOPPED SPINACH
1 CUP CHOPPED MUSHROOMS

PROCESS

1. IN A PROCESSOR, BLEND ALL THE CRUST INGREDIENTS UNTIL IT COMES TOGETHER.

2. I USE TWO MINI PIE TINS TO MAKE MINI QUICHES OR YOU COULD USE A STANDARD 10 OR 12 INCH PIE PAN AS WELL (IF YOU CHOOSE THIS THE TIME FOR YOUR QUICHE FILLING TO FULLY DEHYDRATE WILL BE LONGER THAN IF YOU DO THE MINI PIES). LINE WHATEVER TIN/PAN YOU CHOOSE WITH WAX PAPER SO YOU CAN PULL THE BASE OUT EASILY.

3. PLACE IN THE DEHYDRATOR AT 115F FOR 4 HOURS (THE SAME TEMPERATURE AS ANYTHING ELSE).

4. WHILE THATS DEHYDRATING, TOSS THE FILLING INGREDIENTS IN A BLENDER AND BLEND UP UNTIL REALLY WELL COMBINED.

5. THEN FOLD IN SPINACH AND MUSHROOMS

6. POUR THE FILLING MIXTURE INTO YOUR ALREADY DEHYDRATED QUICHE CRUSTS. AND PLACE BACK IN THE DEHYDRATOR FOR 8 HOURS OR UNTIL SET.

Banana Cinnamon Rolls

+ PREP TIME
15 MINUTES

+ SERVINGS
6 PEOPLE

+ DEHYDRATE
8 HOURS + 8 HOURS

INGREDIENTS

12 RIPE (BUT NOT TOO RIPE!) BANANAS
1 CUP PITTED DATES
2 TSPS CINNAMON

PROCESS

1. CUT YOUR BANANAS IN HALF LENGTH WISE AND DEHYDRATE FOR 8 HOURS AT 115F.

2. PREPARE A DATE SAUCE BY BLENDING THE DATES + 3/4 CUP WATER AND CINNAMON.

3. LATHER THAT MIXTURE ON THE SEMI-DEHYDRATED BANANAS AND ROLL THEM UP. I ROLL UP HALF A BANANA AND THEN ANOTHER HALF AROUND THE FIRST. SO ONE FULL BANANA PER ROLL.

4. DEHYDRATE FOR ANOTHER 8-10 HOURS AND THEY'RE PERFECT! GOOEY AND SWEET AND WONDERFUL.

Raw Onion Bread

+ PREP TIME	+ SERVINGS	+ DEHYDRATE
15 MINUTES	4 PEOPLE	4 HOURS + 4 HOURS

INGREDIENTS

IN A BLENDER:
1 LARGE SWEET ONION
1/2 CUP YELLOW BELL PEPPER
2 CLOVES OF GARLIC
DASH OF SALT (OPTIONAL)

IN A SEPARATE BOWL ADD:
2 CUPS ALMOND FLOUR (OR CHICKPEA FLOUR)
2 CUPS FLAX MEAL

PROCESS

1. TOSS THE INGREDIENTS IN A BLENDER AND BLEND UNTIL IT'S MOSTLY CHUNK-FREE.

2. ADD YOUR OTHER INGREDIENTS IN A SEPERATE BOWL WITH THE ONION MIXTURE YOU JUST BLENDED.

3. MIX IT ALL TOGETHER. THEN TRANSFER TO A NONSTICK DEHYDRATOR SHEET. WET YOUR HANDS TO KEEP THE MIXTURE FROM STICKING TO YOU TOO MUCH AND PRESS IT OUT FLAT (ABOUT 1/4IN THICK).

4. THEN POP IN THE DEHYDRATOR AT 115F FOR ABOUT 4 HOURS.

5. THEN FLIP IT OFF. SCORE IN SIZE AND SLICES OF BREAD YOU WANT.

6. THEN PUT BACK IN THE DEHYDRATOR FOR ANOTHER 3-4 HOURS.

Grawnola *(Raw Vegan Granola)*

+ SERVINGS
6 PEOPLE

+ PREP TIME
15 MINUTES

+ DEHYDRATE
5 HOURS

INGREDIENTS

IN A FOOD PROCESSOR:
1 TBSP FLAX SEEDS
1 TBSP CHIA SEEDS
1 TBSP HEMP SEEDS
2 CUPS ORGANIC QUICK OATS
1/2 CUP SHREDDED COCONUT
1 TSP CINNAMON
PINCH OF SALT

THEN ADD:
30 DEGLET DATES (OR ABOUT 15
MEDJOOL DATES INSTEAD)

PROCESS

1. ADD YOUR INGREDIENTS INTO A FOOD PRO-
    CESSOR AND BLEND UNTIL REALLY WEL COM-
    BINED.

2. THEN ADD DEGELET DATES AND PROCESS
    AGAIN UNTIL EVERYTHING COMES TOGETHER.

3. IF IT'S NOT PULLING TOGETHER IT'S BECAUSE
    THE DATES AREN'T MOIST ENOUGH SO JUST
    SLOWLY ADD SOME WATER INTO THE FOOD
    PROCESSOR UNTIL IT'S CLUMPING TOGETHER.

4. THEN ADD IN WHATEVER DRIED FRUIT OR
    OTHER ITEMS YOU LIKE (DRIED MULBERRIES,
    BANANAS, CACAO NIBS—JUST TO NAME A FEW
    OPTIONS).

5. DEHYDRATE AT 115F FOR 5 HOURS OR UNTIL
    DRY!

Beet Burger

+ SERVINGS
5 PEOPLE

+ PREP TIME
20 MINUTES

+ DEHYDRATE
6 HOURS

INGREDIENTS

2 CUPS CHOPPED BEETS
1 LARGE CARROTS
1 STALK OF CELERY
2 TBSP CHIA SEEDS
1 TBSP GROUND GINGER
1 TSP GARLIC POWDER
2 TSP PSYLLIUM HUSK
1/2 TSP SALT

PROCESS

1.   ROUGHLY CHOP AND TOSS EVERYTHING IN A FOOD PROCESSOR EXCEPT THE PSYLLIUM HUSK.

2.   ONCE EVERYTHING IS WELL COMBINED--FINELY CHOPPED BUT STILL MAINTAINING SOME TEXTURE-- ADD IN THE PSYLLIUM HUSK. MIX AGAIN UNTIL THAT'S THOROUGHLY MIXED IN.

3.   SEPARATE INTO FIVE EQUAL SIZED PORTIONS AND FORM INTO PATTIES WITH YOUR HANDS. PLACE ON A NONSTICK DEHYDRATOR SHEET AND DEHYDRATE AT 115F FOR 3 HOURS.

4.   THEN TAKE THE PATTIES OFF THE NONSTICK SHEET AND DEHYDRATE AGAIN FOR ANOTHER 3-4 HOURS.

5.   AFTER THAT THEY'RE DONE AND READY TO BE STUFFED IN A WRAP, BETWEEN SOME SLICES OF RAW ONION BREAD OR TOPPED ON A SALAD!

Raw Vegan Pizza

+ SERVINGS	+ PREP TIME	+ DEHYDRATE
4 PEOPLE	**30 MINUTES**	**15 HOURS**

INGREDIENTS

FOR THE CRUST:
1 1/2 CUPS GROUND FLAX
1 CUP WATER
3 CLOVES OF GARLIC
2 MEDIUM/LARGE PEELED ZUCCHINI
2 TBSP ITALIAN SEASONING
DASH OF SALT (OPTIONAL)

FOR THE SAUCE:
1 PINT OF TOMATOES
8 DEGLET DATES
2 TSP CURRY POWDER
1 TBSP PIZZA SEASONING
1/4 CUP SUNDRIED TOMATOES
DASH OF WATER TO BLEND
1 MEDIUM/LARGE ZUCCHINI

THEN ADD YOUR FAVORITE TOPPINGS:
(THINK IN A VARIETY OF COLORS!)
2 CUPS CHOPPED KALE
1/2 CUP CHOPPED ONIONS
1 CUP SLICED MUSHROOMS
1/2 A LARGE ORANGE BELL PEPPER
RAW MOZZARELLA
PIZZA SEASONING
CHILI FLAKES
DRIED THYME

PROCESS

1. FOR THE CRUST: BLEND EVERYTHING ON HIGH SPEED UNTIL IT'S VERY WELL COMBINED. IT SHOULD BE THICK.

2. SPREAD EVENLY ONTO NON STICK DEHYDRATOR SHEETS. DEHYDRATE FOR ABOUT 6 HOURS AT 115F

3. THEN FLIP THE CRUST OFF THE NONSTICK SHEETS SHEETS AND DEHYDRATE FOR ANOTHER 8 HOURS OR UNTIL DRY (DRYING TIME WILL VARY DEPENDING ON HOW THICK YOU SPREAD THE CRUST). DEHYDRATE UNTIL THE CRUST IS DRY BUT NOT TOUGH OR CRUNCHY.

4. FOR THE SAUCE: BLEND IT ALL UP AND THEN SPREAD ON YOUR PIZZA CRUST (WHEN READY!)

5. THEN ADD YOUR FAVORITE TOPPINGS (THINK IN A VARIETY OF COLORS!)

6. AND FINALLY YOUR SEASONINGS ON TOP: SPRINKLE OF PIZZA SEASONING, SPRINKLE OF CHILI FLAKES, AND SPRINKLE OF DRIED THYME!

7. POP IT ALL IN THE DEHYDRATOR FOR A FINAL MESHING OF FLAVORS (1-2 HOURS) AND THEN ENJOY!

Sprouted Chickpea Burger

+ SERVINGS
6 PEOPLE

+ PREP TIME
30 MINUTES

+ DEHYDRATE
6 HOURS

PROCESS

1. START BY SOAKING ABOUT 1 CUP OF CHICKPEAS FOR 2 DAYS (THE CHICKPEAS GROW A LOT!)

2. ONCE THE CHICKPEAS ARE READY TO GO START BY MAKING YOUR CHIA EGG AND ALLOWING TO SIT FOR 5 MINUTES OR SO.

3. TOSS THE CHICKPEAS IN A FOOD PROCESSOR WITH EVERYTHING BESIDES THE CHIA EGG AND ALMOND FLOUR. PROCESS UNTIL WELL COMBINED.

4. ONCE IT'S ALL WELL COMBINED TAKE THE CHIA EGG AND ALMOND FLOUR AND TOSS IT IN WITH EVERYTHING ELSE. COMBINE IT THROUGHLY WITH YOUR HANDS.

5. FORM INTO PATTIES (I USUALLY GET ABOUT 6 BURGERS OUT OF THIS RECIPE). DEHYDRATE AT 115F FOR 6 HOURS AND THEN DONE!

INGREDIENTS

3 CUPS OF SPROUTED CHICKPEAS
3 CLOVES OF GARLIC
1 SMALL ONION
2 TEASPOONS CORIANDER
3 TEASPOONS CUMIN
2 TABLESPOONS OF TAHINI
3 TBSP DRIED PARSLEY
1 TBSP DRIED BASIL
DASH OF SALT
CHIA "EGG"
(1 TBSP CHIA SEEDS + 3 TBSP OF WATER)
3 TABLESPOON OF ALMOND FLOUR

Teriyaki Burger

+ SERVINGS   + PREP TIME   + DEHYDRATE
5 PEOPLE   20 MINUTES   10 HOURS

INGREDIENTS

FOR THE BURGER:
2 CUPS MUSHROOMS
1 CUP CARROTS
1 CUP CELERY
2 CLOVES OF GARLIC
DASH OF SALT
2 TSP ONION POWDER
3/4 CUP SOAKED WALNUTS
(OR SUNFLOWER SEEDS)
1/2 TBSP PSYLLIUM HUSK POWDER

TERIYAKI SAUCE:
3 TBSP TAHINI
2 TBSP COCONUT AMINOS
2 CLOVES OF GARLIC
10 DEGLET DATES
1 TBSP MAPLE SYRUP
CHUNK OF GINGER THE SIZE OF YOUR
THUMBNAIL
1 TSP PAPRIKA
ADD WATER TO BLEND

PROCESS

1. BLEND/PROCESS THE BURGER INGREDIENTS UNTIL IT'S WELL COMBINED BUT STILL HAS SOME TEX-
    TURE AND CHUNKS. YOU DON'T WANT MUSH. THEN ADD IN 1 1/2 TBSP PSYLLIUM HUSK BLEND AGAIN
    TO COMBINE. FOLD IN HALF OF THE TERIYAKI SAUCE.

2. FORM INTO PATTIES (I MADE 5 OUT OF THIS RECIPE—THEY SHRINK QUITE A BIT AFTER THEY'RE DE-
    HYDRATED). PLACE ON A NONSTICK SHEET FOR YOUR DEHYDRATOR, AND DEHYDRATE AT 115F FOR
    ABOUT 10 HOURS (FLIPPING THEM OFF THE NONSTICK SHEET AFTER 3 HOURS OR SO).

3. I PLACED MY BURGER ON A BED OF SPINACH, TOPPED WITH THE REST OF THE TERIYAKI SAUCE, TO-
    MATOES, ONIONS, SESAME SEEDS, CHILI FLAKES AND DRIED PARSLEY AND DONE.

Taco Pizza

+ SERVINGS
4 PEOPLE

+ PREP TIME
15 MINUTES

INGREDIENTS

TOP YOUR PIZZA CRUST WITH
MARINARA SAUCE:
2 CUPS FRESH TOMATOS
8 DEGLET DATES
1/4 CUP SUNDRIED TOMATOES
PINCH OF SALT
DASH OF WATER TO BLEND

THEN ADD CARROT TACO "MEAT" AND PICO!

PROCESS

1. DEHYDRATE FOR 2-3 HOURS.

2. THEN PULL OUT OF THE DEHYDRATOR AND SPREAD A LAYER OF YOUR SPROUTED ALMOND SOUR CREAM, SOME SMALL CHUNKS OF AVOCADO, A SPRINKLE OF FRESH CILANTRO, AND (IF YOU CAN HANDLE IT) SOME CHILI FLAKES!

3. AS ALWAYS, GET CREATIVE AND ADD WHATEVER TOPPINGS/SAUCES/ETC YOU LOVE! HAVE FUN WITH IT!

Onion Rings

+ SERVINGS
2 PEOPLE

+ PREP TIME
25 MINUTES

+ DEHYDRATE
5-6 HOURS

INGREDIENTS

1 LARGE SWEET ONION
2 CUPS GROUND FLAX SEEDS
1 TBSP ONION POWDER
1 TBSP GARLIC POWDER
2 TBSP DRIED PARSLEY
2 TSP SMOKED PAPRIKA
1 TSP SALT
2 TBSP APPLE CIDER VINEGAR

PROCESS

1. CUT ONION INTO 1/2 INCH THICK SLICES. DIP THE SLICES INTO THE APPLE CIDER VINEGAR (YOU COULD ALSO USE LEMON JUICE FOR THIS IF YOU PREFER)

2. COMBINE HALF OF ALL THE DRY INGREDIENTS TOGETHER (I FIND IT'S MUCH EASIER TO MAKE TWO SEPARATE BATCHES TO PREVENT THE BREADING FROM CLUMPING UP TOO MUCH AND BECOMING DIFFICULT TO COAT THE ONION).

3. ROLL THE ONIONS IN THE BREADING AND PLACE ON A DEHYDRATOR SHEET AND DEHYDRATE FOR 5-6 HOURS.

Tiki Masala Cauliflower Wings

+ SERVINGS
2 PEOPLE

+ PREP TIME
30 MINUTES

+ DEHYDRATE
4 HOURS

INGREDIENTS

1 SMALL HEAD OF CAULIFLOWER

FOR THE SAUCE:
1 1/2 CUPS TOMATOES 2 TBSP TAHINI
6 DEGLET DATES 2 CLOVES OF GARLIC
1 THUMBNAIL SIZED PIECE OF GINGER
1 TSP GARAM MASALA
1 TSP TURMERIC POWDER 1 TSP CUMIN
1/2 TSP PAPRIKA DASH OF SALT
1/2 CUP WATER

PROCESS

1. CHOP UP ONE SMALL HEAD OF CAULI-
    FLOWER INTO BITE SIZED BITS (ABOUT
    5ISH CUPS WORTH)

2. BLEND ALL THE SAUCE INGREDIENTS

3. THEN POUR OVER THE CAULIFLOWER
    AND COAT THOROUGHLY.

4. PLACE THE CAULIFLOWER EVENLY ON A
    DEHYDRATOR SHEET AND TOSS IN THE
    DEHYDRATOR AT 115F FOR 4 HOURS.

Curry Walnut Burger

+ SERVINGS
4 PEOPLE

+ PREP TIME
20 MINUTES

+ DEHYDRATE
8 HOURS

INGREDIENTS

1 CUP CHOPPED CARROTS
1 CUP SOAKED WALNUTS
1 ROMA TOMATO
1 TBSP CURRY POWDER
1 TSP GINGER
DASH OF SALT
2 TBSP GROUND FLAX

PROCESS

1. PULSE IN THE BLENDER UNTIL WELL COMBINED SO YOU CAN FORM PATTIES.

2. DIVIDE THE MIXTURE INTO 4 PATTIES (OR MORE IF YOU WANT THEM SMALLER) AND PLACE ON A NONSTICK SHEET IN THE DEHYDRATOR FOR 4 HOURS.

3. THEN FLIP THEM OFF THE SILICONE SHEET AND DEHYDRATE AGAIN FOR ANOTHER 4 HOURS.

4. STUFF IN A WRAP OR TOP ON A SALAD--THESE GO GREAT IN SOME NORI SHEETS AS WELL!

Chili Burger

+ SERVINGS
5 PEOPLE

+ PREP TIME
30 MINUTES

+ DEHYDRATE
7 HOURS

INGREDIENTS

2 LARGE CARROTS
2 STALKS OF CELERY
1 CUP OF CHERRY TOMATOES
3 DEGLET DATES (OR 1 MEDJOOL)
1/4 CUP SUNDRIED TOMATOES
1 TSP GARLIC POWDER
1 TSP CHILI POWDER
2 TSP SMOKED PAPRIKA
2 TBSP GROUND FLAX
2 TSP PSYLLIUM HUSK
1 TSP SALT (OPTIONAL)

PROCESS

1. ROUGHLY CHOP AND TOSS EVERYTHING IN A FOOD PROCESSOR/BLENDER EXCEPT THE PSYLLIUM HUSK.

2. ONCE EVERYTHING IS WELL COMBINED--FINELY CHOPPED BUT STILL MAINTAINING SOME TEXTURE-- ADD IN THE PSYLLIUM. MIX AGAIN UNTIL THAT'S THOROUGHLY MIXED IN.

3. SEPARATE INTO FIVE EQUAL SIZED PORTIONS AND FORM INTO PATTIES WITH YOUR HANDS. PLACE ON A NONSTICK DEHYDRATOR SHEET AND DEHYDRATE AT 115F FOR 3 HOURS.

4. THEN TAKE THE PATTIES OFF THE NONSTICK SHEET AND DEHYDRATE AGAIN FOR ANOTHER 3-4 HOURS (DEHYDRATING TIME MAY VARY A BIT BASED ON YOUR PREFERENCE/SIZE OF BURGERS.

Pizza Rolls

+ SERVINGS
2 PEOPLE

+ PREP TIME
20 MINUTES

+ DEHYDRATE
13 HOURS

INGREDIENTS

FOR THE "DOUGH":
2 EARS OF CORN
1 MEDIUM PEELED ZUCCHINIS
3 CLOVES OF GARLIC
1 TBSP APPLE CIDER VINEGAR
1/2 TSP CORIANDER
1/2 TSP CUMIN
DASH OF SALT
3 TBSP PSYLLIUM HUSK

FOR THE SAUCE:
1 CUP TOMATOES
2 CLOVES OF GARLIC
6 DEGLET DATES
1 TBSP APPLE CIDER VINEGAR
1 TBSP OREGANO

PROCESS

1. FOR THE DOUGH, THROW EVERYTHING IN A BLENDER EXCEPT THE PSYLLIUM HUSK. BLEND WELL AND THEN ADD THE PSYLLIUM HUSK AND BLEND AGAIN ON HIGH SPEED FOR 30 SECONDS.

2. SPREAD ALL THE BATTER ON A NONSTICK SHEET. DEHYDRATE AT 115F FOR 3 HOURS AND THEN FLIP AND DEHYDRATE FOR ANOTHER 3-4 HOURS.

3. FOR THE SAUCE, BLEND ALL THAT TOGETHER AND SPREAD EVENLY ON YOUR PIZZA ROLLS BASE. I LIKE TO ADD ONIONS AND MUSHROOMS TO MINE AS WELL BUT USE WHATEVER VEGGIES YOU LOVE FOR FILLING--OR DON'T USE ANY VEGGIES AT ALL!

4. DEHYDRATE AGAIN FOR ANOTHER 5 HOURS. ONCE THE SAUCE IS MOSTLY DEHYDRATED ROLL THEM UP!

5. YOU CAN POP THEM BACK IN THE DEHYDRATOR FOR ANOTHER COUPLE HOURS TO FIRM UP, OR IF YOU'RE IMPATIENT YOU CAN GO AHEAD AND EAT IT RIGHT AWAY! I DO SUGGEST GIVING IT ANOTHER 2 HOURS IN THE DEHYDRATOR SO THEY STAY TOGETHER A BIT BETTER, THOUGH.

RAW VEGAN
Desserts

Peanut Butter Chocolate Energy Balls

+ SERVINGS
6-8 PEOPLE

+ PREP TIME
20 MINUTES

INGREDIENTS

IN A FOOD PROCESSOR ADD:
3 CUPS OATS
2 TBSP CACAO POWDER
DASH OF SALT (OPTIONAL)
3 CUPS PITTED DATES

THEN ADD:
3 TBSP PEANUT BUTTER

PROCESS

1. PROCESS EVERYTHING EXCEPT THE
    PEANUT BUTTER UNTIL WELL COMBINED

2. THEN ADD PEANUT BUTTER, PROCESS
    AGAIN AND, IF NEED BE, ADD A TOUCH
    OF WATER (1/3 CUP OR LESS) SLOWLY
    JUST UNTIL THE MIXTURE STARTS TO
    COME TOGETHER INTO A "DOUGH".

3. ROLL INTO LITTLE, INDIVIDUAL BALLS
    AND ENJOY!

Oatmeal Raisin Cookies

+ SERVINGS	+ PREP TIME	+ DEHYDRATE TIME
6 PEOPLE	20 MINUTES	3-4 HOURS

INGREDIENTS

IN A BOWL ADD:
1 CUP OATS
1 CUP ALMOND FLOUR
1 CUP RAISINS
1 TSP CINNAMON

IN A BLENDER MIX:
3/4 CUP WATER
25 DEGLET DATES
1 1/2 TBSP ALMOND BUTTER
DASH OF SALT

PROCESS

1. BLEND DATES, ALMOND BUTTER, SALT AND WATER UNTIL WELL COMBINED.

2. THEN POUR OVER THE BOWL OF DRY INGREDIENTS. MIX REALLY WELL.

3. SPOON THEM ONTO A NONSTICK DE-HYDRATOR SHEET. DEHYDRATE FOR 3 HOURS AT 115F AND DONE!

Mint Chocolate Chip Ice Cream

+ SERVINGS
2 PEOPLE

+ PREP TIME
15 MINUTES

INGREDIENTS

5 FROZEN BANANAS
4 MEDJOOL DATES
1/2 CUP PACKED WITH MINT LEAVES
(OR JUST 1 DROP OF A FOOD-SAFE MINT
ESSENTIAL OIL! BE CAREFUL WITH THIS
STUFF; IT'S POTENT!)
HANDFUL OF FRESH SPINACH
(OR MY FAVORITE DAILY GREEN BOOST
POWDER)

PROCESS

1.   BLEND IT ALL UP!

2.   THEN FOLD IN OR TOP WITH 1 TBSP
     OF CACAO NIBS.

Chocolate Pudding Pie

+ SERVINGS
6-8 PEOPLE

+ PREP TIME
15 MINUTES

+ SET TIME
2 HOURS

INGREDIENTS

FOR THE CRUST:
1 1/2 CUPS DATES
1 1/2 CUPS SOAKED ALMONDS
2 TBSP CACAO POWDER

FOR THE FILLING:
6 LARGE RIPE HASS AVOCADOS
1 CUP CACAO POWDER
1 1/2 CUPS MAPLE SYRUP

PROCESS

1. IN A FOOD PROCESSOR, PULSE CRUST INGREDIENTS UNTIL WELL COMBINED AND PRESS INTO A PIE PAN (I LIKE TO LINE MINE WITH WAX OR PARCHMENT PAPER SO I CAN PULL THE PIE OUT MORE EASILY ONCE IT'S READY

2. THEN BLEND THE FILLING INGREDIENTS UNTIL IT'S NICE AND SMOOTH AND THEN POUR ON TOP OF THE CRUST.

3. STICK IT IN THE FREEZER FOR AN HOUR OR TWO TO FIRM IT UP. THAT'S IT! THIS IS A TOTAL CLASSIC SO SIMPLE BUT NOTHING LIKE A RICH, DECADENT CHOCOLATE PIE, RIGHT?!

Raw Vegan Linzer Cookies

+ SERVINGS
6 PEOPLE

+ PREP TIME
25 MINUTES

+ DEHYDRATE
4-5 HOURS

INGREDIENTS

IN A LARGE BOWL COMBINE:
2 1/2 CUPS ALMOND FLOUR
1/4 TSP SALT
1 CUP RAW COCONUT SUGAR
1 1/2 TSP LEMON ZEST
MIX THAT UP REALLY WELL.

THEN ADD:
1 CUP OF RAW COCONUT BUTTER (MANNA)
3 TBSP WATER

TOP WITH:
RASPBERRIES
BLUEBERRIES
LEMON ZEST

PROCESS

1. BEGIN TO MIX EVERYTHING TOGETHER WITH YOUR HANDS BEING SURE TO CRUMBLE THE COCONUT BUTTER INTO TINY PIECES. CONTINUE TO WORK IT UNTIL IT ALL STARTS TO PULL TOGETHER INTO A DOUGH BALL.IF YOU NEED TO, ADD A FEW MORE TBSPS OF WATER TO HELP IT ALONG.

2. ONCE IT'S ALL COME TOGETHER AND NOT TOO CRUMBLY PLACE IN THE FRIDGE TO SIT FOR AN HOUR.

3. AFTER AN HOUR OR SO PULL IT OUT AND AT THIS POINT YOU COULD ROLL IT OUT WITH A ROLLING PIN AND MAKE COOKIE CUTTER COOKIES. I CHOSE TO JUST PULL PIECES OF DOUGH APART AND ROLL THEM INTO BALLS WITH MY HANDS. THEN I WOULD PRESS A SMALL INDENT INTO THE MIDDLE WHERE I PUT MY FRUIT. THE FRUIT IS JUST A COMBINATION OF SMASHED RASPBERRIES, BLUEBERRIES AND A TOUCH MORE OF LEMON ZEST (ABOUT 1/4 CUP EACH OF THE BERRIES).

4. PLACE ON A DEHYDRATOR SHEET AND DEHYDRATE AT 115F FOR 4 HOURS AND DONE.

5. *NOTE: THE COOKIES MIGHT NOT SEEM DONE WHEN THEY ARE IN FACT DONE BECAUSE COCONUT BUTTER IS SOFT WHEN WARM. ONCE THESE SIT OUT OF THE DEHYDRATOR AND COME UP TO ROOM TEMPERATURE THEY'LL FIRM UP SOME MORE.

Raw Banana Bread

+ SERVINGS
8 PEOPLE

+ PREP TIME
20 MINUTES

+ DEHYDRATE
7-9 HOURS

INGREDIENTS

IN A BLENDER TOSS:
25 DEGLET DATES
2 BANANAS
4OZ WATER

IN A SEPARATE BOWL COMBINE:
3 CUPS OATS
2 CUPS ALMOND FLOUR
2 TSP CINNAMON
1/2 TSP SALT

PROCESS

1. BLEND DATES, BANANA AND WATER UNTIL WELL COMBINED.

2. MIX THAT TOGETHER THEN DUMP THE BANANA/DATE MIXTURE ON TOP OF DRY INGREDIENTS AND MIX TOGETHER UNTIL IT'S NICE AND COMBINED.

3. FORM INTO A "LOAF" HOWEVER YOU WANT, PLACE ON A NONSTICK DEHY-DRATOR SHEET. SLICE A BANANA IN HALF AND STUFF IT IN THE TOP. AND POP IN THE DEHYDRATOR AT 115F FOR 7-9 HOURS (DEPENDING ON HOW EXACTLY YOU SHAPE YOUR LOAF).

INGREDIENTS

FOR THE CRUST:
2 CUPS ALMONDS
PINCH OF SALT
3/4 CUP DATES

FOR THE FILLING:
2 CUPS SOAKED MACADAMIA NUTS (OR CASHEWS IF YOU PREFER)
2 CUPS PEELED PUMPKIN
1 CUP MAPLE SYRUP
JUICE OF 1 LARGE LEMON
3 TBSP COCONUT CREAM
1 TBSP PUMPKIN PIE SPICE
1 TSP CINNAMON
DASH OF SALT

Pumpkin Pie

+ SERVINGS	+ PREP TIME	+ SET TIME
6-8 PEOPLE	25 MINUTES	4 HOURS

PROCESS

1. TOSS THE ALMONDS IN THE FOOD PROCESSOR AND PROCESS UNTIL IT'S A FLOUR.

2. THEN ADD THE DATES AND SALT AND PROCESS AGAIN UNTIL WELL COMBINED AND STARTS TO COME TOGETHER IN A "BALL". IF YOU NEED TO ADD JUST A TABLESPOON OR TWO OF WATER TO THOROUGHLY COMBINE THINGS.

3. ONCE COMBINED PRESS INTO A WAX PAPER LINED SPRINGFORM PAN.

4. BLEND ALL THE FILLING INGREDIENTS UP UNTIL IT'S SUPER SMOOTH AND CREAMY.

5. POUR OVER THE CRUST AND ALLOW TO SET IN THE FREEZER FOR ABOUT 4 HOURS.

Raw Vegan Carrot Cake

+ PREP TIME
30 MINUTES

+ SERVINGS
6-8 PEOPLE

+ SET TIME
3 HOURS

INGREDIENTS

FOR THE FILLING
IN A FOOD PROCESSOR ADD:
4 CUPS SHREDDED CARROTS
3 CUPS PITTED DATES

2 CUPS WALNUTS
1/4 TSP SALT
2 TSP CINNAMON
1/2 TSP NUTMEG
1 TSP GROUND GINGER

THEN ADD:
1/2 CUP ALMOND FLOUR
1/2 CUP RAISINS

FOR THE FROSTING
PLACE IN A BLENDER:
1 CUP MACADAMIA NUTS (OR CASHEWS!)
1/2 CUP COCONUT CREAM
3 TBSP LIGHT MAPLE SYRUP
3 TBSP LEMON JUICE

PROCESS

1. *FRIENDLY REMINDER TO ALWAYS SOAK YOUR NUTS/SEEDS (IDEALLY OVERNIGHT) BEFORE USE*

2. START BY GRATING 4 CUPS OF CARROTS EITHER WITH A HAND GRATER OR WITH A FOOD PROCESSOR. THEN REMOVE CARROTS AND PLACE IN A SEPARATE BOWL.

3. THEN IN THE FOOD PROCESSOR PLACE 3 CUPS OF PITTED DATES. PROCESS THAT UNTIL IT COMES TOGETHER IN A SORT OF "DOUGH BALL". PLACE IN A LARGE BOWL WITH THE GRATED/SHREDDED CARROTS.

4. PROCESS WALNUTS AND SPICES UNTIL WELL COMBINED THEN ADD BACK IN THE DATES AND CARROTS TO THE FOOD PROCESSOR AND COMBINE IT ALL.

5. ONCE THAT'S ALL COMBINED TRANSFER BACK TO YOUR LARGE BOWL (I KNOW: A LOT OF TRANSFERRING BACK AND FORTH–BUT IT'S FOR CREATING THE PERFECTLY TEXTURED CAKE!).

6. THEN ADD 1/2 CUP ALMOND FLOUR AND 1/2 CUP RAISINS. STIR IT ALL TOGETHER WITH YOUR HANDS

7. PRESS INTO A SPRINGFORM PAN WITH WAX PAPER ON THE BOTTOM. PLACE IT IN THE FREEZER TO SET.

8. BLEND FROSTING INGREDIENTS UNTIL SUPER SMOOTH! POUR OVER THE BASE AND ALLOW TO SET IN THE FREEZER FOR SEVERAL HOURS UNTIL FIRM!

9. GARNISH HOWEVER YOU WANT! I LIKE TO ADD SOME SHREDDED CARROTS AND CARROT RIBBONS AROUND THE EDGES. A FEW SPRIGS OF FRESH MINT. AND A SPRINKLE OF CINNAMON ON TOP. GET CREATIVE AND ENJOY!

Lemon Bars

+ PREP TIME
20 MINUTES

+ SERVINGS
6-8 PEOPLE

+ SET TIME
3 HOURS

INGREDIENTS

FOR THE CRUST
IN A FOOD PROCESSOR ADD:
2 CUP OATS (OR ALMONDS)
2 TBSP MAPLE SYRUP
5 DEGLET DATES
2 TBSP WATER
DASH OF SALT

FOR THE FILLING
IN A BLENDER ADD:
1 CUP SHREDDED COCONUT (OR
CASHEWS OR MACADAMIA NUTS).
1 CUP COCONUT CREAM
1/2 CUP LEMON JUICE
1 TBSP LEMON ZEST
1/4 CUP MAPLE SYRUP
PINCH OF SALT

PROCESS

1. BLEND/PROCESS CRUST INGREDIENTS YOU UNTIL IT PULLS TOGETHER AND ISN'T CRUMBLY (IF IT IS CRUMBLY SIMPLY ADD MORE WATER OR MAPLE SYRUP).

2. PRESS INTO A WAX PAPER LINED DISH. (WETTING YOUR HAND OR UTENSIL TO PRESS INTO THE DISH MAKES THINGS SO MUCH EASIER/LESS STICKY)

3. BLEND ALL THE FILLING INGREDIENTS UP UNTIL IT'S NICE AND SMOOTH.

4. THEN POUR OVER THE CRUST AND PLACE IN THE FREEZER FOR A FEW HOURS UNTIL IT'S SET.

5. I ADDED A SLICE OF LEMON TO THE TOP (JUST FOR THE PICTURE) AND SOME ADDITIONAL ZEST AND COCONUT FLAKES.

Key Lime Pie

+ PREP TIME	+ SERVINGS	+ SET TIME
25 MINUTES	6-8 PEOPLE	3 HOURS

INGREDIENTS

FOR THE CRUST
IN A FOOD PROCESSOR ADD:
1 CUP ALMONDS
1 CUP UNSWEETENED SHREDDED COCONUT
1 CUP PITTED DATES

FOR THE FILLING:
IN A BLENDER ADD:
5 LARGE HASS AVOCADOS
1 1/4 CUP MAPLE SYRUP
1 CUP LIME JUICE

PROCESS

1. PULSE THE CRUST INGREDIENTS IN A FOOD PROCESSOR UNTIL WELL COMBINED AND THEN PRESS INTO A SMALL PIE PAN (OR A CUPCAKE TIN FOR MINI-PIES!).

2. BLEND THE FILLING INGREDIENTS UP REALLY WELL! I RECOMMEND GIVING IT A TASTE BEFORE FILLING THE CRUST. SINCE AVOCADO SIZES VARY AND SUCH YOU MIGHT WANT TO ADD A TOUCH MORE LIME JUICE OR MAPLE SYRUP TO ADJUST IT TO YOUR PREFERENCE.

3. PLACE IT IN THE FREEZER TO SET FOR 3 HOURS AND THEN ENJOY!

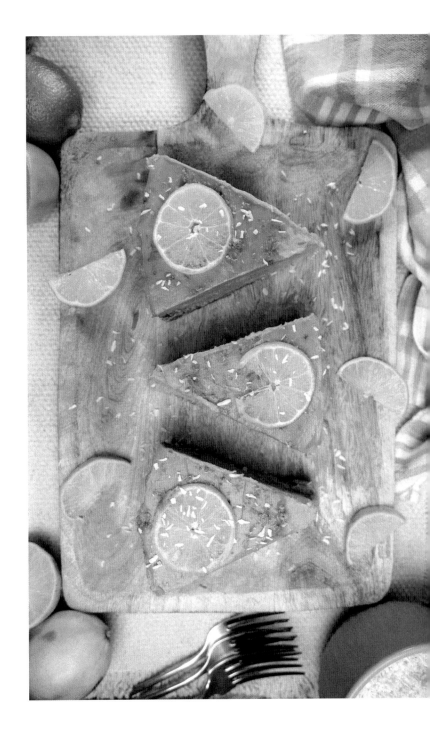

Banana Creme Pie

+ PREP TIME
25 MINUTES

+ SERVINGS
6-8 PEOPLE

+ SET TIME
3-4 HOURS

INGREDIENTS

FOR THE CRUST
IN A FOOD PROCESSOR ADD:
1 CUP SOAKED ALMONDS
1 CUP DATES

FOR THE FILLING
IN A BLENDER ADD:
2 BANANAS
1 CUP SOAKED MACADAMIA NUTS
HALF A CAN OF COCONUT CREAM
(ABOUT 7 OUNCES)
1/3 CUP MAPLE SYRUP
2 TBSP LEMON JUICE
DASH OF SALT

PROCESS

1. BLEND CRUST INGREDIENTS UNTIL WELL
   COMBINED AND THEN PRESS INTO A PAN
   LINED WITH WAX PAPER.

2. BLEND FILLING INGREDIENTS UNTIL
   REALLY SMOOTH THEN POUR OVER
   YOUR CRUST AND POP IN THE FREEZER
   OVERNIGHT OR UNTIL SET.

3. I DECORATED MINE WITH SOME FRESH
   BANANAS AROUND THE EDGE AND A
   SPRINKLE OF CINNAMON. AND DONE!

Raw Vegan Apple Pie

+ SERVINGS
6-8 PEOPLE

+ PREP TIME
30 MINUTES

+ DEHYDRATE
3 HOURS (OPTIONAL)

INGREDIENTS

FOR THE CRUST TOSS IN A FOOD PROCESSOR:
3 CUPS DATES
1 CUP DRIED MULBERRIES
1 CUP SPROUTED BUCKWHEAT

FOR THE FILLING TOSS IN A BLENDER:
2 APPLES
2 CUPS OF DATES
2 TSP APPLE PIE SPICE
(OR 1 TSP CINNAMON PLUS 1 TSP ALL SPICE)
DASH OF SALT
DASH OF WATER IF YOU NEED IT TO BLEND

5 LARGE APPLES

PROCESS

1. PROCESS ALL THE CRUST INGREDIENTS UNTIL IT ALL PULLS TOGETHER (YOU MAY NEED TO ADD A TOUCH OF WATER). THEN PRESS IT INTO A PIE PAN.

2. BLEND ALL THE FILLING INGREDIENTS UP TILL NICE AND SMOOTH AND THICK. THIS IS YOUR DATE SAUCE.

3. FINELY CHOP (OR GRATE) 5 LARGE APPLES. ON TOP OF THE CRUST LAY OUT YOUR APPLE SLICES, THEN A LAYER OF THE DATE SAUCE, THEN ANOTHER LAYER OF APPLES, SAUCE, ETC UNTIL YOU'VE USED UP ALL YOUR APPLES AND SAUCE.

4. I TOPPED MINE WITH SOME EXTRA DRIED MULBERRIES FOR THAT CRUNCHY TOPPING AND A DASH OF CINNAMON.

5. YOU CAN EAT IT AS IS. I POPPED MINE IN THE DEHYDRATOR FOR 3 HOURS TO WARM UP BUT IF YOU DON'T HAVE A DEHYDRATOR OR DON'T WANT TO WAIT FOR THIS STEP THAT'S FINE TOO!

Snickerdoodle Cookies

+ SERVINGS
6 PEOPLE

+ PREP TIME
20 MINUTES

INGREDIENTS

½ CUP FLAX SEEDS (OR GROUND FLAX TO MAKE EVEN EASIER)
1/2 CUP CHIA SEEDS
2 CUPS UNSWEETENED SHREDDED COCONUT
12 PITTED MEDJOOL DATES
1 TSP. CINNAMON POWDER

PROCESS

1. IN A FOOD PROCESSOR COMBINE THE FLAX, CHIA, CINNAMON, AND COCONUT. PROCESS UNTIL ITS A FINE POWDER.

2. THEN ADD THE DATES. PROCESS AGAIN UNTIL IT ALL FORMS INTO A SORT OF BALL. YOU MAY WANT TO ADD JUST THE TINIEST BIT OF WATER IF IT ISN'T COMING TOGETHER EASILY.

3. FORM INTO BALLS AND THEN PRESS A FORK INTO THE TOP OF THEM TO GIVE THEM THAT CLASSIC COOKIE AESTHETIC. AND DONE!

Chocolate Donuts

+ SERVINGS
8 PEOPLE

+ PREP TIME
25 MINUTES

+ DEHYDRATE
6 HOURS

INGREDIENTS

1.5 CUPS OF SOAKED RAW ALMONDS
(I SOAK OVER NIGHT)
2 CUPS PITTED DATES
2 TBSP CACAO POWDER
1 TBSP RAW ALMOND BUTTER
1 TSP SALT (OPTIONAL)

PROCESS

1. FIRST TOSS ALL THE ALMONDS (DRAINED ALMONDS) IN A FOOD PROCESSOR AND PROCESS UNTIL SMOOTH.

2. THEN ADD THE REST OF THE INGREDIENTS AND PROCESS UNTIL WELL COMBINED.

3. ROLL INTO BALLS, FLATTEN THEM OUT AND POKE YOUR FINGER THROUGH TO CREATE LITTLE DONUTS.

4. THEN PLACE ON A DEHYDRATOR SHEET. DEHYDRATE THEM FOR 6 HOURS.

Made in United States
Orlando, FL
21 August 2024

50630455R00044